INSTANT CREDIBILITY

A Simple 5-Step System To Be KNOWN As

"THE EXPERT"

In Your Field; Grow Your Business; Make More Money; And Have The Life You Always Dreamed Of

BY:

David DeSchoolmeester

5-Time Amazon #1 Best Selling Author

Certified Business Performance Coach

THIS PAGE INTENTIONALLY LEFT BLANK

I dedicate this revision to the Love Of My Life

My wife – Wendy!

Revision published by D14 Coaching LLC

Copyright © January 8, 2024, 2022, 2019

D14 Coaching LLC Websites:

- https://D14Coaching.com – Main business "HUB" website.
- https://SaaS.D14Coaching.com – D14 (SAAS) Software-As-A-Service Packages
- https://ABotForYou.com – ChatBot Site
- https://ForeverPractice.com – coming soon: D14 Coaching 9-Step Membership Training Portal
- https://GrabSuccessNow.com – coming soon

FREE BOT BONUS!

R2D14 Super-Bot

FREE Website Chatbot

With the purchase of any sized D14 Software Package!

1. Just go to https://d14coaching.com/freebot
2. Follow the instructions.
3. Get Your FREE Website Chatbot!

TABLE OF CONTENTS

WHO IS THIS BOOK FOR

OVERVIEW

DISCLAIMER

PREFACE

STEP 1 – CONTINUE THE CONVERSATION

STEP 2 – HAVE SOMETHING YOUR COMPETITION DOES NOT

STEP 3 – DO SOMETHING YOUR COMPETITION IS NOT DOING

STEP 4 – USE SOCIAL MEDIA

STEP 5 – USE AMAZON TO YOUR ADVANTAGE

BONUS – PROTECTING YOUR REPUTATION ONLINE

INCREDIBLE OFFER!!!!!!!

OTHER BOOKS BY DAVID

WHO IS THIS BOOK FOR

This book is written to help a very specific audience. One who will find this book extremely helpful to the growth of their practice and/or business and provide for more of a life at home with your family.

If you are part of this audience –

this is a MUST-READ book!

This book represents many years of hard work, experience and effort by numerous Marketing Firms and Marketing Experts who have come before me!

Here is what to expect in this book so you get the most out of it and your expectations are met.

First, this book is for Medical Private Practice Owners and Service Business Owners. It's intended to help you grow your practice/business, produce qualified leads, build authority, create instant credibility and make a long lasting practice providing generational wealth.

Second, it's for IMPLEMENTERS. If you're the type who's looking for free, easy money, this isn't the book for you. I'm not here to blow smoke up your butt and lie to you. There is no such thing as free, easy money. This will take work, but the payoff is HUGE!

Third, this is a book that's short, but packed with easily implementable content and lots of ideas. My intention and the purpose of this book is to show you the most powerful way to market yourself, generate qualified leads, become known as the EXPERT in your field, and set yourself up for long-term growth.

I'll be the first to admit, I'm a shameless self-promoter - and I want to help you reach more people, make more money and add value to your life and everyone you encounter!

Having said that, if you like what you read, *or most of what you read*, I'd absolutely, positively love to hear from you, get to know you better and have you post a success story, picture or video and comment on my Facebook wall at www.facebook.com/d14coaching/

It's my pleasure to help you make money, change lives and gain more freedom!

Sincerely,

David DeSchoolmeester, Long Beach, MS, USA

PS - If you love this book or make money because of it, will you please post a review on Amazon? Your support makes a difference and I read all the reviews personally so I can make this book even better. If you

DON'T like it, send me an email, tell me why and I'll give you your money back, fair enough?

Thank you again for your support!

OVERVIEW

What is Instant Credibility and how will it change the way you do business?

Every Professional need's a consistent flow of patients, but does not have additional time to put into getting them. They also have to overcome numerous challenges!

How many of the following issues sound like you…?

You Don't:

✓ Have a good plan to consistently bring in new clients

✓ Have a plan to get great speaking engagements

✓ Have a long-term program to keep your business top of mind with your prospects and clients

✓ Have the means to make your business recession proof

✓ Know where to find high-quality, qualified prospects

Instant Credibility is the solution for all of these challenges, and MORE!

With Instant Credibility you can:

- Consistently bring in new prospects and patients

- Find high-quality, motivated prospective patients with money

- Get great speaking engagements where you present your services to many qualified prospective patients at one time

- Build Authority and Credibility making it a "NO BRAINER" for prospects to choose you over your competition

- Easily create a Network of people who will gladly refer prospective patients to you

- Quickly and easily have weeks of videos, audios and blog articles ready to post to YouTube, your own Podcast and your own Blog

Instant Credibility is a very simple book with POWERFUL tools that can make HUGE advances in your practice!

I know this all sounds confusing and amazing at the same time! However, I assure you, it's not confusing at all.

One tool can accomplish all this and more for you and your practice!

Now, who am I and why should you listen to or trust me?

I have had several "issues" causing me to completely change my career path throughout the years.

Here are the two major ones that brought me to where I am today…

- I became disabled while serving my country, causing me to leave the US Navy before I was ready;
- I had a very lengthy illness a few years ago that took away much of what I hold dear.

Money Loves Speed. Time Kills Deals.

With what I'm about to share with you, I can practically guarantee you'll get engagement, responses and action nearly 100% of the time.

So, don't stop here!

Keep reading and get ready to get more patients!

EARNINGS AND INCOME DISCLAIMER:

D14 Coaching LLC cannot and does not make any guarantees about your ability to get results or earn any money with our ideas, information, tools, or strategies in this book. The main thing we cannot control is whether you decide to implement the ideas in the manner it is taught. Therefore, we do NOT guarantee any results you may or may not have.

Nothing in this book, any of our websites, or any of our content or curriculum is a promise or guarantee of results or future earnings, and we do not offer any legal, medical, tax or other professional advice.

Any financial numbers referenced here, or on any of our sites, are illustrative of concepts only and should not be considered average earnings, exact earnings, or promises for actual or future performance.

Use caution and always consult your accountant, lawyer or professional advisor before acting on this or any information related to a lifestyle change or your business or finances. You alone are responsible and accountable for your decisions, actions and results in life, and by your reading this book you agree not to attempt to hold us liable for your decisions, actions or results, at any time, under any circumstance.

PREFACE

Allow me to start this with the following story...

A few years ago I went to lunch with an old friend. For the sake of this story, his name is Eugene. He is a Personal Injury Attorney in a Middle-American city with an average population of 391,500 people.

It was a beautiful spring day, so we sat out in the courtyard, next to a fountain.

Me: "Gene, hello, how are you and the family", I said as we met and sat down.

Eugene: "Fine David, Marie is great, and the kids are both in college."

Me: "So, why did you invite me to lunch? And you are paying, right?" I said laughing.

Eugene: "Absolutely, I'm paying! I need some advice. I know you help businesses grow past problems, seen and unseen, to be successful. Is that right?"

Me: "Yes", as we both ordered our lunch.

Eugene: "David, I never thought I would ever need help in my business, but I do now. I seem to be stagnating and can't find my way out of it. Business is good, but it's not growing, and I could use some of your advice."

Me: "Gene, sooner or later every business runs into this kind of situation at one time or another. And you shouldn't look at needing advice as any kind of failure on your end. You sound very upset at yourself for needing this."

As I continued, the waiter brought our drinks.

Me: "Think about it this way. Every superstar sports player has hired a personal 'Coach' to help them be the very best they can be. That's kind of what I do for those business owners who come to me for help. Think of me as a partner in your business who guides you through rough spots, provides an ear to bounce ideas off of, and sees things in your blind spots that you might not see."

Me: "Now Gene, tell me what's happening today in your business and where you would like to see things 12 months from now."

Eugene: "Okay. I've been in business at the same location for about 8 years now. Each year I have had some increase, sometimes big and sometimes small, but always an increase."

Me: "You know that's unusual to have a steady increase for 8 years, right?"

Eugene: "Yes, but that's just what happened. Except for the last two years. They have been relatively even with this year looking to be the same. I am grossing around $358,000 per year."

"However, there is another Personal Injury Attorney right across the street from me who I have been beating every year until now. How do I get back on track?"

Me: "Okay, well Gene, let's start with finishing what I asked in the first place. The second part was where do you want to be 12 months from now?"

Eugene: "Oh yes, well, I would like to have a steady influx of 2 to 5 new clients per month and be on track to make more than $600,000 in the following year."

As I thought about this, the waiter brought our food. So, we took the time to eat and just made small talk during lunch.

Once we finished and the plates were taken away, I knew I would have Gene's complete focus as I began to lay out a plan for him.

Me: "Gene, let's first look at your website." As I pulled it up, I was not surprised to see that it looked very much like many other attorney websites I have seen.

"Okay, the first thing I see is that you do not continue the conversation."

Eugene: "What conversation?"

Me: "Well, think about it. Most people who go to Google and search for anything, have a conversation going on in their head. It goes something like this... 'I was in a car wreck and need a great attorney'. Now, their search may only be 'personal injury lawyer', but they had a specific issue in mind."

"Your website home page is all about you, your education, where you were born and raised, how many years you've been in business. That's NOT going to get you listed very highly in their search, if at all!"

"You need to talk about your potential client, what kind of accident they may have had and how you can help them. Remember, it's all about THEM – not you."

"To get your business moving and growing again, you need to build 'Instant Credibility' in your field! People need to see you as THE Expert when it comes to Personal Injury."

"Gene, there are over 583 Personal Injury Attorney's in our fair city and only a handful of them have the money to 'Rule The Airwaves' with television and radio ads on all the prime time shows."

"So, that means the rest of you have to find a way to beat out each other for the rest of the business. You DO NOT have the money to beat the 'Big Guys/Gals' at their own game. Therefore, you need to find a way to GET NOTICED!"

"Gene, I'm about to tell you the best way to compete with all of these other attorneys and WIN!"

Eugene: "That's why I came to you Dave, let's hear it!"

Me: "Okay. There are really 5 major steps to Instant Credibility and being 'Known' as THE Expert in your field."

"Here they are:

1. Continue the Conversation
2. Have Something Your Competition Does Not Have
3. Do Something Your Competition Does Not Do
4. Use Social Media to Your Benefit – Better Than Your Competition
5. Use Amazon to Your Advantage"

Eugene: "Dave, what does all of that mean?"

Me: "Well, we're going to need more time. Can you make more time for this conversation?"

Eugene: "Yes, how about Thursday? I'll block off the whole afternoon for this!"

Me: "Very good! I'll see you then and we'll go over each item one step at a time."

Eugene: "Goodbye Dave, I'll see you Thursday at my office."

If you don't mind, I'm going to leave the "story telling" theme in the Preface and just go on to explain the steps I explained to Gene for the rest of the book.

Story telling is fun, but it takes up more words and time. Your time is precious, and I refuse to waste any more of it.

So, from now on, I'll continue with just the facts that you grabbed this book to read.

STEP 1 – CONTINUE THE CONVERSATION

You're probably asking yourself, "What conversation?". Well, when people perform a search on Google, they type in some words and hit the "search" key.

The "conversation" starts with the words they type in looking for your services. In "Internet Marketing" speak, these words are called "Keywords".

Here is a simple three-step process…

FIRST:

Your job is to think about all the keywords that individuals might use to find your business. So, let's look at a brief example…

Again, I'll stick with the vocation we started with in our story. You are a Personal Injury Attorney. The keywords that individuals might use would be (this list is a small sample and is NOT all inclusive):

- Personal Injury Lawyer
- Personal Injury
- Accident Attorney
- Car Accident

- Auto Accident
- Fire
- And many more

So, now you have a list of potential keywords. (Please get a much larger list before going to the next section.) These keywords are important because you want to know how people will be searching for your skills and you want to end up on the list of websites they will have to look at from that search!

SECOND:

The home page of your website should NOT be about YOU!

I repeat – Your home page should NOT be about YOU!

This is where most professional websites make their biggest mistake. So many Professionals' website home page has all the background information about their firm or themselves (personally owned business).

These websites have their name, contact information, schools attended, post-graduate schools attended, awards won, previous work experience, etc.

WARNING – THIS IS WRONG!

Your website home page should include posts, articles, or statements that include the keywords on your list!

This is one major way the Search Engines, like Google, find your website and match you up with the search keywords the individual used. This is how you want potential clients to find you!

I know, you're asking yourself, "Don't I want people to know my education and experience?". **YES**, absolutely! However, you need to do it on another page on your website.

The best place to do this is a page you might call "About Us" or "The Team".

NEVER ON THE FIRST PAGE – "Home Page"

Now, by putting the posts, articles, or statements discussing the keywords from your list, you will be providing information (value) that they are looking for. This will be greatly appreciated by the people who visit your website.

Now for the final step!

LAST:

Give your website visitor something of great value for FREE!

Give them a checklist, helpful article, book, etc. that they can download from your website. Have it listed in a sidebar on your website home page.

This download must be very pertinent to what they are searching for and the services you provide.

My top recommendation is a short book that helps them immediately.

For example, again let's say you are a personal injury attorney who specializes in auto accidents caused by big trucks. If you create a short book like: "You've been in a Big Rig accident, now what?"

You make the book all about the steps they should take to get proper health care and get appropriate legal assistance. Of course, you put a handy checklist in the back of the book to simplify exactly what steps they need to take.

In this checklist you make sure that it covers all the services that you provide.

Have you ever heard the old saying: "People don't care how much you know, until they know how much you care."?

This is very true. Don't worry about giving away this information. When they realize the VALUE they are getting at no cost to them, they will realize how much you care and most will come back to you for assistance.

This is called reciprocity. You did something for them, gave them something of value, they feel like they owe you at least a consultation.

This will produce a client who will trust you before you even open your mouth to talk to them. You will have instant credibility with them before they sit down in your office for the first consultation.

This is a client who will trust you and be loyal to you for a long time to come – as long as you do nothing to make them not trust you.

Well, let's continue the conversation!

This one thing, alone, can make a huge difference in your business today.

This is also a service that many Search Engine Optimization companies and "wanna-be's" charge thousands of dollars to do for you.

This keyword work is a free bonus I provide my clients when they work with me.

Let's go to Step 2!

STEP 2 – HAVE SOMETHING YOUR COMPETITION DOES NOT

A POSITIONING TOOL:

Well, just what is a Positioning Tool? First let's look at what market position or market positioning is.

One definition is (dictionary.com): An effort to influence consumer perception of a brand or product relative to the perception of competing brands or products. Its objective is to occupy a clear, unique, and advantageous **position** in the consumer's mind.

What about Positioning Strategy?

Definition (dictionary.com): How you differentiate your product or service from that of your competitors and then determine which market niche to fill. **Positioning** helps establish your product(s) or service(s) identity within the eyes of the purchaser.

In order to position yourself as a clear market leader and be recognized as the "**Go-To Expert**" in your field, you must have a tool that creates Celebrity Authority for you.

Having Authority in someone else's eyes is like this... For instance, a Doctor, Lawyer, Surgeon, CPA, Dentist, etc, when compared to the average person without those skills is definitely viewed as an Authority.

This also goes for a Plumber, Electrician, Welder, Carpenter... the list is endless. When compared to anyone without special skills, those with the skills can be viewed as an Authority.

But how does one stand out among their peers?

For instance, there may be as many as 500, or more, General Practitioners in a city with 500,000 people. So, how does one General Practitioner stand out among his or her competition?

When comparing one Doctor to another Doctor with the same training, neither, AND both, can be considered an Authority. So, I'll ask again, how does one stand out as the "**Obvious**" choice among all their competition?

Answer... By having a Positioning Tool that creates incredible Celebrity Authority others just do NOT have!

The top two tools that do exactly that are...

1. A Best-Selling Book

2. Great Speaking Engagements

There are others, but none of the other tools have nearly the same power as the first two I just listed. And I listed them in order of importance!

For conversation speak, here are the other positioning tools...

- A Popular Podcast Show
- A Popular YouTube Channel
- A Popular Blog

Without a doubt, the #1 Positioning Tool that creates incredible Celebrity Authority is a Best-Selling Book!

Nothing else even comes close!

Here's how I found this out, strictly by accident...

Several years ago, I became very ill, and it took three years for the doctors to not only figure out what was wrong but find a treatment that worked and helped me get better again.

During that time, I lost A LOT!

- I lost my position at work…I went from leading an office of 42 people and managing a $78 Million budget to answering the phone and signing for packages;
- I lost the respect of my peers as they saw my career crumble down around me;
- My business failed;
- My family began to distance themselves from me (instead of comforting me), and to top it all off…
- My wife decided that "…in sickness and in health…" was not an oath she was willing to stick around for and she left me.

Later, when the doctors figured it out and finally came up with a treatment that put me on the path to be well again, my best friend (an old Navy buddy of mine), said he still heard a lot of depression in my voice and recommended I write about everything that happened. Then to take what I wrote, crumple it up and throw it in the fire in my fireplace. He felt it would be good therapy to get it all out and on paper.

He was right!

When I read what I wrote, I knew others needed to read this and that my story could help them. I just couldn't burn up something that could help others where no one helped me.

So, I published my book and it wasn't long before people began to Google me to find my email and phone number to contact me and ask me all kinds of questions, as though I were a doctor.

I couldn't believe it! My book became a #1 Best Seller on Amazon!

Of course, I told everyone I wasn't a doctor and to contact a professional for advice, but that I would answer their questions based on what happened to me.

Right there I learned the **Power of Positioning!**

So, then I learned everything I could about creating books and making them a Best-Seller on purpose. I expanded my education to all sorts of marketing, positioning and how to help others become "**THE Authority**" in their industry.

It worked like gangbusters and today I have a good business helping more than 80 others achieve #1 Best-Seller status and have Four #1 Best Selling Books of my own to show for it! (Five #1 Books when this book achieved that status!)

The #2 positioning tool is getting great speaking engagements. The best thing is that the Book is the best way to get great speaking engagements!

Here's my own example…

I have Four #1 Best-Selling Books, my latest being "The Authority Maker". (Before this book became my 5th #1 Amazon Best Selling Book). We were going on vacation to St. Petersburg, Florida for my daughters High School Graduation gift and got "permission", from my wife, to work 2 of the 10 days we were there.

So, I made five phone calls and got three speaking gigs, all because of my #1 Best-Seller status with "The Authority Maker". All I had to do was to mention that I have a #1 Best-Selling book and ask if their business group would like me to come and speak about it to their members. I will give you the exact script I used to get Speaking Engagements in a later chapter.

Here's a great article by one of my mentors, Mike Koenigs:

Why Authoring a Book is So Important

Here's why writing a book for your business is so important. First of all, your book equals access, income, and power. It also gives you that additional gravitas, the authority, expert status, and a voice. It's like getting an exclusive **VIP ticket** to a private, members only club.

It helps you become competition-proof and recession-proof. It gives you access to CEOs, VIP's, the media, and celebrities. It allows you to bypass the formalities and get down into business with what I call a Perfect Package.

What do I mean by a Perfect Package?

When you have a book cover made and you get to say, "Here's what it is and here's what it's for," people remember you.

In this day and age with social media and texting and every other doodad going on, something physical that has value, is remembered.

A book can take on multiple forms. It can be a Kindle book. It can be an audio book. It can also become a roadmap for your entire social media broadcast message that you may have.

But, it definitely is something that I take with me everywhere I go.

I've always got 3-4 copies of my book and a handy-dandy Sharpie pen everywhere I go, ready to introduce myself to anyone that I want to connect with.

Published Authors Make More Money and Help More People!

Your book is about gaining access to an exclusive, member's only club; meeting with CEOs and celebrities; getting VIP treatment; gaining instant credibility; garnering speaking opportunities; and attracting media attention.

It's about getting paid what you're worth, not what you can get.

It's an opportunity to make more, live more, and give more.

- - - - - End of article.

I help my personal clients create an incredible book that provides strong influence and positioning. You go from Zero to having a Best-Selling Book in **less than 90 days!**

Your book creates the content to share and spread throughout the Internet via your Podcast, YouTube Channel, and Blog I help you create as well.

Here are just a few examples of people who had businesses that weren't quite going as well as they hoped. Then they **"Authored"** a book, and their business took off!

BECAUSE OF MY BOOK!

Andy Falco-Jimenez

An ex K9 cop that retired and started a business training K9's for the police.

Because of his book he...

- Got a speaking engagement at Caesar's Palace
- Got a speaking engagement at Planet Hollywood
- Spoke in front of the National Press Corps
- Got a gig on National Geographic
- Was interviewed on ABC News
- Was on Discovery Channel

Because of his National Geographic appearance, Andy was called by a Saudi Arabian Prince and picked up a $750,000 contract training dogs for the Prince.

And it all started with his #1 Best-Selling Book.

Ed Rush

Ed is an Ex U.S. Marine Fighter Pilot who left the military and began his own marketing firm focusing on Attorneys.

Ed tried to speak at Bar Associations to build credibility. The first year he was only able to get one speaking engagement.

He then wrote a #1 Best-Selling book called "Turn Clicks Into Clients", again, focused on Attorneys.

The following year he had 48 speaking engagements at Bar Associations all around the country because he used his book to get them.

In three short years he turned his company into a $1M per year business.

He used his book to get in the door. It's a great Authority and Credibility tool!

Abbey Richter

A 9-year-old girl, whose parents own a Veterinary Hospital, wrote FOUR #1 Best-Selling books on pets.

She has been interviewed on TV and in magazines.

She has also made over $30,000 in speaking fees in just one year!

Don't let age stop you, there is no reason you cannot do this!

John Cote

John wrote a book about marketing. This brought him an opportunity for a free speaking gig.

From that he got two consulting deals with doctors for $12,000.

From that he received a call for a speaking engagement at an event for Medical Tourism. He didn't know anything about it but did a bunch of studying and decided there was a great opportunity there.

So, he began a Podcast where he interviewed physicians and patients about Medical Tourism and how helpful it really is for specific patients.

He was then called back to the original place that hired him to speak at their Medical Tourism event for free. Only this time he was paid as the "Keynote Speaker"!

He then turned that Podcast into a Book on Medical Tourism.

Now, because of his Podcast and his new Book on Medical Tourism, he received a call from the Minister of the country of Belize. That call resulted in a deal for $250,000 with the country of Belize!

John continues to do more consulting in this area and works with others on developing books about Medical Tourism for $30,000 each for his clients!

Today, every "Big-Time" marketer uses books to introduce themselves, their products, ideas, and their ability to solve your problems.

Books are, without a doubt, the BEST door opener, Authority Maker and Credibility Builder!

There is nothing else that works better than a book!

So, let's get back to the chapter…

Many people get scared off when they think about "writing" a book. That's because we were all lead to believe myths that just aren't true.

[**NOTE**: With my system, my clients don't "write" a book, they "Author" a book that is their words, their thoughts – but without the "writing" part!]

These myths have kept thousands of people from getting their thoughts published and helping others with their ideas. I was one of them, until I learned that they just weren't true.

Please allow me to explain…

Myth #1: It Takes Too Long

We've all seen interviews with famous novelists that claim "…this was 20 years of my life…". That's why we all THINK it takes years and years to get a book from our mind and onto paper.

I'm here to tell you THAT's NOT TRUE!

You can do anything with a good system! And I've got a GREAT one!

Depending on the availability of getting an average of 12 hours from my clients (not all at once), there book can be ready for purchase, in its entirety, in LESS THAN 60-DAYS!

That's right!

I didn't stutter!

From zero to having a book completed in under 2-MONTHS!

Myth #2: It Costs Too Much

That's one I agree with 100%!

You may be thinking… "WHAT?"

The Opportunity Costs of waiting so long to get started are VERY EXPENSIVE!

You've seen already what people can do with their book. And that's just the tip of the iceberg.

There are many, many stories of success just like the ones I've already shared with you!

Let's take a look at an example of an Estate Planning Attorney who averages $3,000 to $4,000 per client.

Now, what if his book cost him $20,000 for the whole project, including a #1 Best-Selling campaign.

So, he uses his book and gets between 1 to 4 new clients per month from it.

Okay, now let's use the example of just 1 new client per month at $4,000.

In 5 months the book would have paid for itself and by the end of the year this Attorney would be up by $28,000!

Here's the math:

($4k x 12 months) = $ 48,000 - $20,000 cost of book leaves him/her with an additional $28,000.

AND

The book keeps working month after month!

If there were 4 new clients each month the profits from the first year alone would be an **ADDITIONAL $ 172,000!**

So, what if you wait a year!

Would that have been expensive!

Yes, you might miss out on a potential windfall!

So, the cost of WAITING IS VERY EXPENSIVE!

Myth #3: What If Someone Else Wrote About My Topic?

I say SO WHAT?!?

Pick any topic and perform a search for that topic in any online bookstore (Amazon, Barnes & Noble, Good Reads, Google Books, etc.). You will find many books on that topic.

Does that mean that only one was successful and the others were not? NO!

Check out the Self-Help section in the library or book store. There are a lot of authors, all with their own twist on each subject.

Besides, the most important thing is "Why" you are authoring this book!

You are NOT authoring your book so that you can become rich on book sales. Your book will be helping you grow your business by giving you **something your competition does NOT have**.

Being an author means you are an **EXPER**T in your field. That will be easily recognized by anyone going to your website and seeing you are a #1 Best-selling author.

At that point, their search is done! They have found the professional they are looking to do business with!

And that is what your book is for!

Publish a book and you'll have a high-quality piece of information to give to all of your prospects. Instead of throwing up a sales letter on a website, you can stand out far beyond your competitors who don't have books.

Bestseller status gives you immediate credibility and authority and positions you as a **go-to** person.

The fact is, this works for any business, anywhere in the world. Thinking that you're "local" is irrelevant as to whether or not a book would be a powerful marketing tool for you.

Something I do for my clients is, I help them create an incredible book that provides strong influence and positioning. You can go from Zero to having a Best-Selling Book in **less than 60 days!**

Your book creates the content to share and spread throughout the Internet via your Podcast, YouTube Channel, Blog and other methods.

This is a process of repurposing content and has many names.

Here are just a few by three of my mentors…

- Viralocity, by Brandon Burchard
- Omni Presence, by Frank Kern
- You Everywhere Now, by Mike Koenigs

The top Internet Marketers use books to Teach First and then present an offer. This includes multi-millionaire marketers like: Frank Kern, Brendon

Burchard, Dean Graziosi, Mike Koenigs, Dan Kennedy, and many more.

Here are some additional client experiences:

The Only Marketing I Do	$1,000,000+ Deal	Shorter Sales Cycle	Increased Visibility
Marketer Ken Matejka found that his best-selling book is the only marketing he needs to do.	Roger Sramek's best-selling book resulted in a venture deal in less than a year from its publication	Paul Svec's best-selling book resulted in faster sales cycles and well-educated (and happy) clients	Attorney Christopher Hanson's videos based on his best-selling book attracted 20,000+ views in less than a year

- Marketer Ken Matejka found that his best-selling book (The Lawyer's Ultimate Guide to Online Leads) is the only marketing he needs to do.

- Roger Sramek's best-selling book (Your Sleep: Wake Up Refreshed!) resulted in a venture deal worth over $1M in less than a year from publication.

- Paul Svec's best-selling book (Make Your Small Business Communications Ecosystem Thrive) resulted in faster sales cycles, well-educated and happy clients.

- Attorney Christopher Hanson's videos based on his best-selling book (A Trial Lawyer's Tales From The Trenches) attracted more than 20,000 views in less than a year.

- Plus: Marketer Rob Cuesta had the following to report in a Facebook Group about his client's book results...
"Had a meeting with one of my clients today who flew in from the UK to discuss his second book (and, as it turned out, a third and fourth) - we ended up talking for four hours as I planned out various new marketing campaigns for him. He attributes $19 MILLION of additional revenue to the first book we ghostwrote for him! And yes, I've asked him for a testimonial!"

The below nine (9) items are a sample of what you need to create an incredible book to promote your business...

1. Compelling Title / Subtitle

We will start with one of the two most important components of your book - the title. Your book title needs to grab attention, accurately describe your book, and get your prospect to open it and read it. Most books never get read. So, think of the title as the "headline" for your book. This process is harder than you might think. Bottom line - it needs to be awesome...and we'll come up with a great one together.

2. Excellent / Brand-Representative Cover

People say, "don't judge a book by its cover." Want to know why they say that? It's because everyone judges a book by its cover! Creating a GREAT cover is the single most important thing you can do with your book. That's because your book can be your #1 selling, branding, and lead generation tool.

Here is an example of my first book that I told you about when I became ill and lost so much in my life. The Title: "SLEEP APNEA DREAM KILLER"; subtitle: "How A Sleep Disorder Nearly Devastated My Life"; and the compelling image. All three together worked incredibly well to get my book to #1 in 2 categories!

3. Book Content

There are 2 ways to get a book done. You can sit down and type it all out. Or I can interview you and we can get the book recorded, transcribed and edited. The first process can take a significant amount of time and the 2nd process a day or two. It's an easy way to get all of the information out of your head and into a book and our team can do all of this with you.

4. Book Web Page

Nothing else sells a book like a great web page. Our team will create something beautiful and brand representative that represents your book so that you can send people there to buy your book. This page directs them to get your book and captures their contact information.

5. Category Selection

Another secret to becoming a number 1 best-seller is choosing the right category(s). This really is the secret sauce. Together, we will choose 1-4 great categories so that you're virtually guaranteed to become a number 1 bestselling author. Each Amazon category lists the top selling books you can check on to see when it moves up to #1.

6. Amazon Author Page

The key to a great online presence for your book is a great Amazon author page. Frankly, most authors and even some of the big New York Times best-selling authors have very poor author pages. Together we'll create a great brand representative author page that you will love and one that will rank you high in the search engines so people can find you there.

7. Launch On Kindle

The first place we launch your book will be on Kindle. Not only is it the fastest way to get published and promoted, but it'll also give you massive immediate exposure to everyone who owns a Kindle, an iPad, or any connected device.

8. Best-Seller Promotion

This is where the rubber meets the road. It doesn't make sense having a book if it's not a best-seller. This is your calling card. Using our proprietary system and methods, we will launch your book in its category to become a # 1 best-seller. It's something you can be proud of for the rest of your life.

9. Launch On Paperback

The next launch is on paperback, so people can go to Amazon, buy it, and use Amazon Prime's 2-day ordering system to get it in their hands. You're also going to want to have your own book as a physical copy, so that you could hand them out at speaking events, or you can use it as a great business card.

Summary

This program represents a strong focus of your marketing dollars into what really works - a book. By the time you're done, you'll have an excellent / brand representative book that you can be proud of.

A Best-Selling Book is the most powerful tool I know for getting new clients and building your business!

Now on to Step 3!

STEP 3 – DO SOMETHING YOUR COMPETITION IS NOT DOING

You've gone to conventions, training seminars and other such peer events. While you were there you talked to your peers. Most of them are doing the same thing to get new clients.

I recommend you take – "the road less travelled". Think out of the box. The professionals who are truly recognized as "The Expert" in their field do things that few professionals do.

But this gets them more publicity, more recognition, a bigger paycheck, increased client flow and more credibility.

Use your book to **build your platform**, **grow your list**, and **monetize customers**. It's also a perfect way to become **competition-proof** and **recession-proof**. Your book is the **perfect tool** to build relationships.

Here are some examples of how your book can build your business…

1) Use Your Book to Get Speaking Gigs

Every one of the speakers I have ever seen at ANY type of "event" was an AUTHOR. Being an author, especially a Best-Selling author is an extremely powerful tool to build your business.

As a matter of fact, I would go so far as to say it's **THE #1 TOOL FOR BUILDING A BUSINESS** beyond yourself!

If you're not much of a speaker, hone your skills by joining Toastmasters and, more importantly, getting small local speaking engagements.

So, how do you get these local speaking engagements? Very simple, I'm glad you asked. Let me give you an example of my own.

A few years ago, we took my youngest daughter to St Petersburg, Florida for a high school graduation trip. There are things that my wife and daughter like to do that I do not.

So, I suggested we take an additional 2 days and they can go off and do what they like, while I speak to some local business owners. My wife agreed, of course.

A few weeks prior to our trip I went onto "meetup.com" (a website where like-minded people join local groups to "meetup" and talk). I joined some Christian Business groups in the St. Petersburg area.

Then I made FIVE (5) phone calls and got THREE (3) speaking engagements. Each event was me talking to no less than 15 local business owners.

You do not have to talk to local business owners. I'm just giving you my example. You can search and find groups of all kinds. Find groups that you feel you could help.

Here's a couple of examples:

ONE: Let's say you are a Psychiatrist/Psychologist or a Licensed Therapist. Look for groups that meet because of a "loss" or another problem.

TWO: Let's say you are a Physician. Look for groups that meet over a specific illness issue or general illness issues that pertain to your specialty.

Okay, now that you know how to find a group, would you like the script I used and still use to get speaking engagements?

I thought you'd never ask.

Once you have found a few groups that you would like to talk to, you contact the owner/manager of the group on "meetup.com". Normally, you are only going to get an email address through "meetup.com". Very rarely will you be able to get a phone number.

It doesn't matter, the script is exactly the same either way. Here's the email you send (just change my specific example to your specialty).

Hi, {first name of owner of the group},

My name is David DeSchoolmeester. I am the Best-Selling author of "Instant Credibility". It teaches business owners how to become known as THE EXPERT in their field to beat out their competition.

I am on a book tour and part of that book tour is a speaking tour. I would love to come in and speak to your group at your next meeting. Of course, this is at no charge, I will be teaching a brief synopsis of what I teach in my book.

Do you think your members would be interested?

You can get back to me at: {email address} or {phone number}.

Thank you in advance for the opportunity to sit down and chat with your group.

Very Respectfully,

David DeSchoolmeester

{Now, if you really want to sweeten the deal you could add a P.S. like this...}

P.S. For everyone who attends the meeting, I will give away a free copy of my Best-Selling book, signed by the author!

You don't have to give away the book. If you feel very strongly that this group has your ideal clients as members, you could give away a free 30-minute session with you one-on-one. You could make the giveaway anything that they would deem of VALUE and is an acceptable cost to you.

The FREE gift almost always locks in the speaking engagement.

NOTE: I made 5 phone calls and booked 3 speaking engagements. The other two groups had speakers coming in already for the time period I was going to be available.

2) How To Reach The Unreachable

Suppose you have a prospect that you have been trying to get an appointment with, but just can't seem to get past the "Gatekeeper" – otherwise known as the Secretary or Executive Assistant.

Here is a method you can use that has an outstanding success rate!

It turns out it's easy to take your book and deliver it to your prospect, gift wrapped and with a card. It's a great way to establish yourself as an expert and authority in your field and get that appointment.

For a few bucks, you can mail your book to this prospect to get your foot in the door... but here's the best strategy to use to bypass the gatekeepers.

I buy my own book on Amazon and have it delivered to a prospect, gift-wrapped, with a card... and Amazon pays me royalties when I buy my own books (happy result)!

When is the last time you ignored a package from Amazon, especially one that is gift-wrapped?

I don't know about you, but I would consider it very rude if my assistant opened up my presents! So, this is how you get past the gatekeeper.

People "meet" you in your book.

You start a one-way conversation with them. You reveal your "reason why" you do what you do in your book, which creates a reason why they're going to do business with you.

Introduce yourself to your prospects with an attention-grabbing book title.

Prior to sending this book to them, you create a very short video (not longer than 3 minutes). In this video you make it personal to them, using their name, introduce yourself and how you can align yourself directly with a specific goal of theirs.

Then request an appointment after they read your book.

Now, in the note you put on the gift, you tell them about the video (on YouTube) that you know they will enjoy and give them the URL to the video.

3) Attend Events With People You Want to Meet

The next way to grow your business is to attend events where people you want to connect with are present.

Let's say, you know that there's going to be a celebrity at a certain event. This is someone you've wanted to connect with for a long time and they're actually going to be at this event. Bring along a few copies of your book and a sharpie.

When you've identified someone that you want to connect with, pull out your book, open it up, find a page that might be most relevant to that person, sign the book with your contact information, and a little note to them.

Walk up to them after they finish speaking, or when you can track them down without being weird, and give them your book.

I've found it's the perfect way to actually connect with people. My mentor (Mike Koenigs) met Richard Dreyfuss because he had a book and a sharpie with him.

He went on to help him get more recognition for his Non-Profit organization.

Richard Dreyfuss and Mike hanging out on Mike's video set.

4) Use Your Book to Get Interviews

The next way you can use your book is to reach out and get interviews on podcasts or other mediums.

There are people dying to interview best-selling authors for their shows. It's a win-win for both of you.

You can give your book away in exchange for a lead when you're being interviewed. You can use the strategies above to actually get the interview in the first place.

5) Prepare a Press Release

As soon as you write your book, no matter what it is, you can prepare a press release. Put that on a site like "prweb.com" or other similar press release companies.

Here's what happens...

As soon as that press release is published, other news outlets like Forbes and Entrepreneur, may pick up the article and post it on their site.

That gives you some additional "link juice" as we like to call it. Those quality links are useful to establish yourself as a credible expert and industry authority, and give you some celebrity status as well.

You can also boost your credibility on your website by posting "as seen on" links back to those articles.

6) Create an Audio Version of Your Book

With nothing more than a USB microphone from Amazon, you can record an audio version of your book.

One favorite is the Blue Yeti. There's also one called the Blue Nessie.

 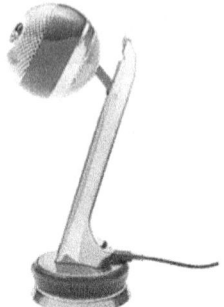

Left: Blue Yeti ($108) and Right: Blue Nessie ($80)

When you upload your audio book you can get free distribution on Audible (an Amazon company), and iTunes. You'll also get paid a healthy commission each time it sells.

Generally, you get about 65% of the price of your audio book as revenue. Another option I've done and highly suggest is putting your audio book up for free as a podcast. Allow iTunes, and the other podcast networks to distribute your content for free.

Don't be afraid of giving away your content.

For example, people who buy books, or audio books, are going to be different than the people who listen to podcasts.

Your goal is to get recognized, be seen, and build your celebrity status.

7) Get Media Gigs

Another way you can use your book is to get media gigs. You can learn how to be effective on camera and then get TV interviews.

Your book is a vehicle. When you're established as a best-selling author, people are going to want to listen to you. You're treated as an authority and an expert.

8) Schedule Webcasts to Discuss Your Book

Schedule webcasts on Blab Zoom, or Google Hangouts, and then promote those opportunities on social media to talk about the content of your book.

You can give away your content and teach it, and then offer your book as a bonus.

9) Create an Information Product Out of Your Book

If you're wondering, how do I sell?

How do I make money?

Consider creating an information product that's based on your book. You can sell it to your existing audience that you have and to the list that your building.

10) Always Give Your Audience a "**Call to Action**"

The other thing that you want to make sure that you have in your book is something called a call to action. A call to action asks people to take a certain action from within your content.

Each call to action is a way to interactively engage the reader and drive them to some kind of bonus or gift.

You can give away:

- Training videos
- A free audiobook
- Surveys
- Trials of your products or services
- A consulting session
- Diagnostics
- A high-value way to get closer and deepen the relationship

The reason you embed a call to action in your book is because publishers (like Amazon and Barnes & Noble) don't give you the contact information of the book buyer. You need the right strategies, tools, and systems to drive readers to your offers and capture leads.

Why a Book is Better Than a Business Card

Using your book to introduce yourself is certainly a creative spin on the old business card.

A book is the best business card to get introduced to practically anyone. Then you need to write inside of your book to get every one of them to remember you.

One of the things I've learned is that giving a book to someone is the single most powerful way to get introduced to them, period!

The $100,000 Sharpie Trick

What's the secret formula to write in the book?

This is the $100,000 Sharpie Trick…

Inside the book cover write this:

"Hi {person's name}, great meeting you today, I have an idea that will _____."

The idea could be:

- Help you make more money.
- Raise money for your foundation.
- Get you more attention.
- Get you in the media.
- Get you in the news.

…whatever it is that you can help someone with.

Then, make it personal…

Write, "Check out page ## inside my book. Because it's something you can use right now. Text me at this number {insert your cell number} or email me {insert your email}. Looking forward to connecting soon."

…and sign it.

Here's what happens.

People remember you.

Everyone is handing out business cards. Everyone has seen a business card.

People throw away business cards.

People don't throw away books.

Books have a lot of value.

Books Sell Your Products and Services Faster and Easier

It's just that simple!

Let's move on…

STEP 4 – USE SOCIAL MEDIA

SOCIAL TOOL:

Being "social" over the Internet has become an incredibly large part of many of our lives. This is why having a strong Social Tool is so important.

You're about to discover a system that will put you on level playing ground with the best of the best in your field and soar above all your peers.

We already know that the most powerful tool in our arsenal is our Best-Selling book. Next was Speaking Engagements. In this chapter we'll talk about the next logical step to continue to build your "Ultimate Authority" over your competition!

Let's start with a very short lesson on communication.

Dr. Albert Mehrabian performed studies to determine the percentages of effective types of communication.

He found that:

- The actual "words" used make up only 7% of effective communication;

- The "vocal elements" (such as tone of voice, voice inflection, etc) make up 38% of effective communication;

- "non-verbal" (such as how you move your hands, the look on your face, your general posture, and much more) make up 55% of effective communication

So we find that if we use just a newsletter or blog, we are achieving only 7% of the potential for effective communication; if we use audio like a podcast, we are achieving 38%; but if we use VIDEO, we achieve 93% of the potential for effective communication.

Now that we know video is the best way to communicate online, let's continue.

Using our book, we make videos based on each chapter. This is relatively easy as the content is already complete. We are simply going to repurpose the same content and distribute it in different locations throughout the Internet.

Look at the following image.

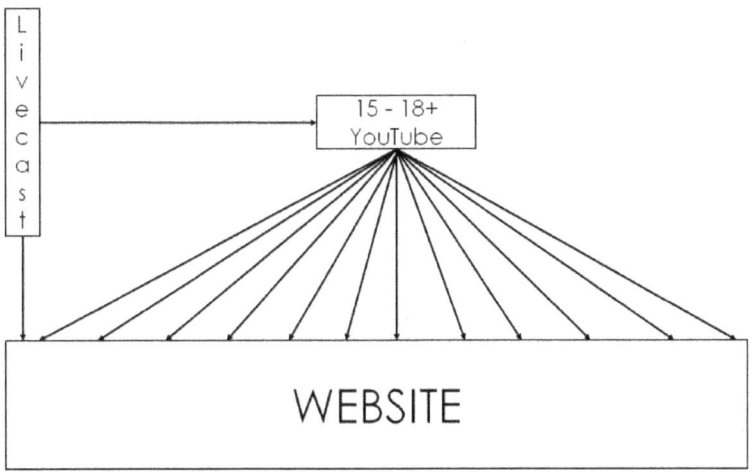

Let's say that in order to create your book I interviewed you to collect all your knowledge into one video file.

Then we cut up that video so that there is a separate video file for every chapter. We edit the chapter videos to include a professional introduction and information at the end letting viewers know how to contact you to get even more information.

I do all of this for each one of my book clients.

As you can see in this first image, we create a YouTube channel for your company and upload the chapter videos. We upload one video each week, so if you have 15 to 18 chapters, you'll have 15 to 18 weeks of uploads.

The arrows from the YouTube uploads represent viewers following the links back to your website, thus driving more traffic to you!

Each one of these videos take no more extra time from you as I create them from our initial book interview recording!

AND each one of these drive traffic to your website and to your business!

There are many other websites where we can upload your videos to – doubling and tripling your social reach!

Video sites are not the only social method of outreach the Internet has to offer!

What about Podcasting? Many people use and prefer Podcasts over YouTube. In fact, many Podcasts are now becoming available on automobile radio systems.

iTunes alone has over 1 Billion customers! That's a huge audience!

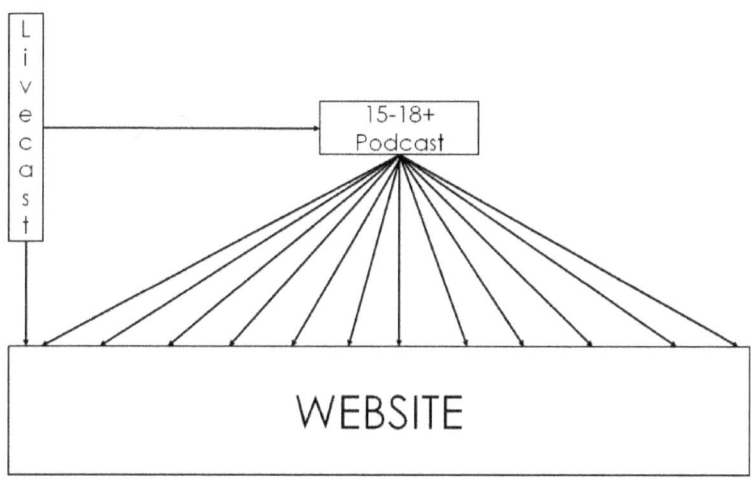

AND now putting them both together.

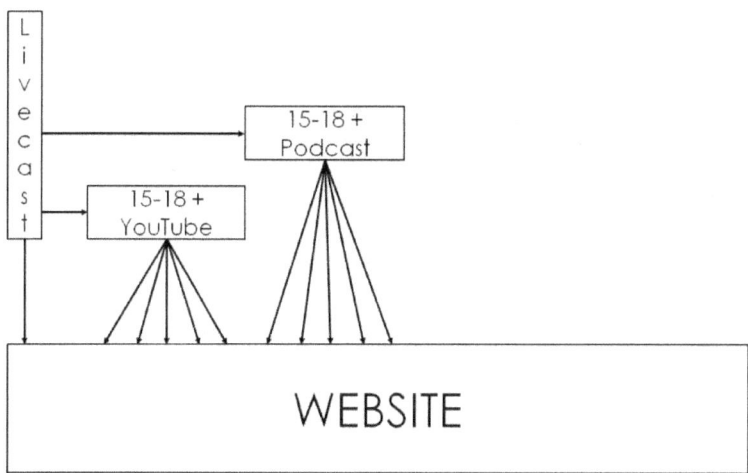

Now let's add your book and its online reach.

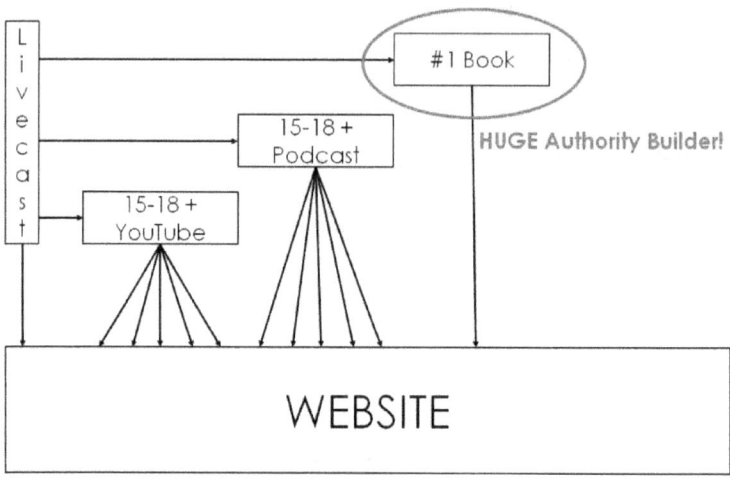

In the next chapter we'll look into how to use your Amazon Author Page. Amazon gives you a webpage (at no cost to you) where you can put all kinds of information about yourself.

So, let's see how that helps your business grow!

For more FREE information, visit:
https://D14Coaching.com

STEP 5 – USE AMAZON TO YOUR ADVANTAGE

Finally Step 5. As I just stated, Amazon gives all of its authors a free webpage where you can not only post your book information, but all kinds of other information.

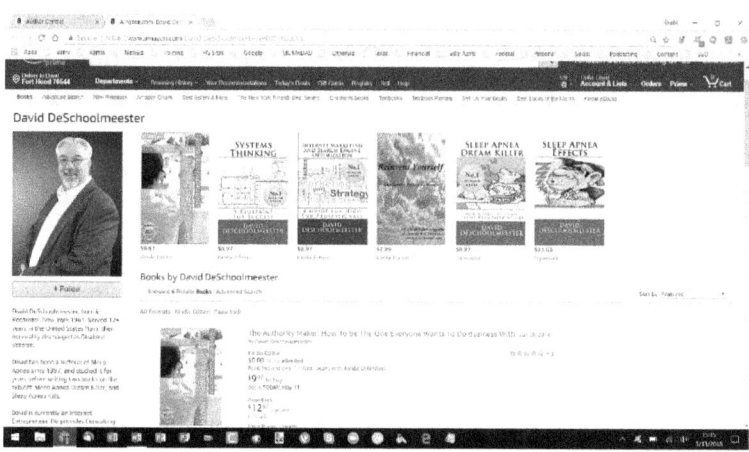

Here is my Author page. The web address is https://amazon.com/author/daviddeschoolmeester/

As you can see, you can list:

- Your Photo
- Your Biography

- All of your books
- Videos
- Podcast posts
- Blog posts
- Business Information
- Calendar of Events
- And more

This is an incredible marketing tool! It's also an incredible Search Engine Optimization (SEO) tool!

Remember, SEO has a great deal to do with links that come back to you or your website from other highly regarded websites. There's no other highly regarded website than Amazon!

SEO is also based on search keywords. For instance, if someone were to do a Google search on my name, my Amazon pages/book pages will show up on the first page of the search results.

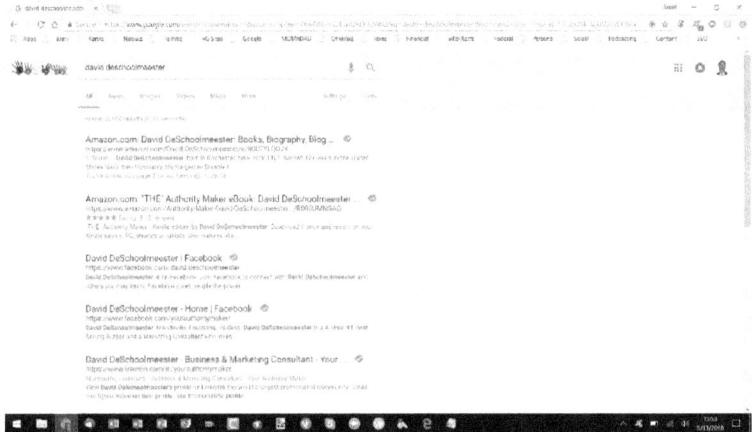

At the very top of the Google search for my name is my Amazon Author Page!

My latest book "The Authority Maker" is #2!

As you can see, your Amazon Author Page is incredibly important for your business! And you get one free, just by having a book!

Here is how the rest of the social media plays out (continuing from the last chapter).

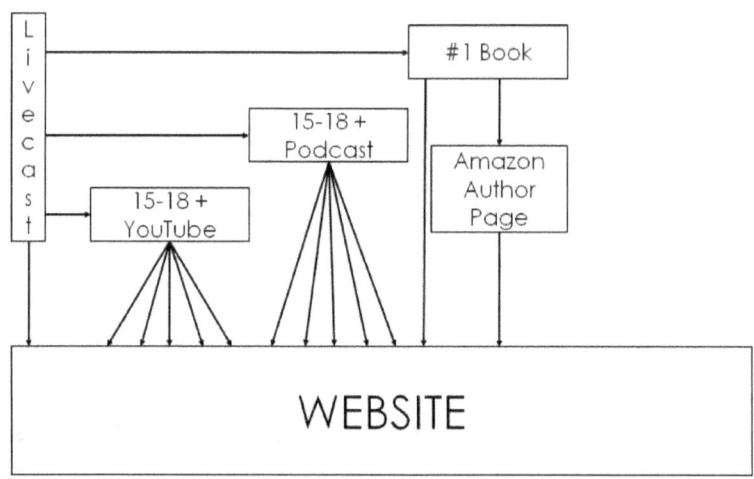

Adding your Amazon Author Page.

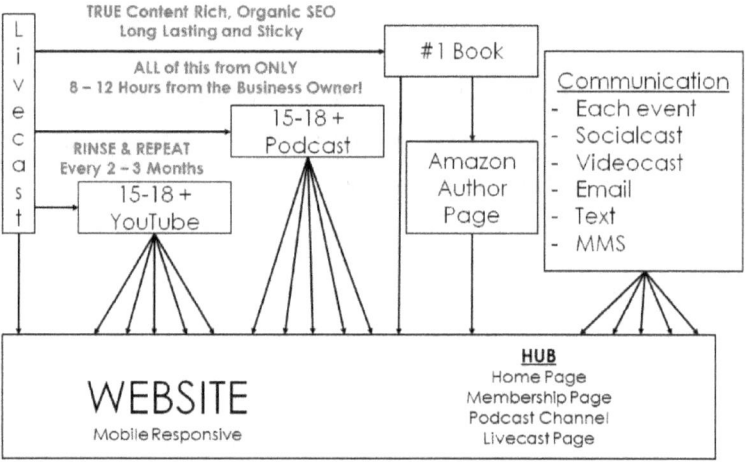

This includes other business communications from you and your business.

All that you see above is an entire marketing program for your business that stems from your

BOOK and just a 12-hour commitment from you – the business owner!

Next is a BONUS chapter for you. Then, "What To Do Next!" Where I have a great offer for you. I hope you enjoyed this book as much as I enjoyed writing it for you.

BONUS – PROTECTING YOUR REPUTATION ONLINE

Reputation Management is heavily overlooked by most small business owners. That's mainly because few people know how to make this work for them. Large businesses & corporations understand the importance of and have several people that work on this each day.

Doctors, Chiropractors, Physicians, etc., you need this to keep a strong flow of prospective patients coming into your office. This is definitely doing something others are NOT doing – so Reputation Management can make an incredible difference to your practice.

It's not just about getting more 5-Star ratings and reviews. It's also about preventing, or at least minimizing, negative reviews.

Here's what a recent search on OpenAI's ChatGPT came up with concerning Business and Reputation Management…

Online reviews are important for businesses because they can have a significant impact on a business's reputation and bottom line. According to a survey conducted by BrightLocal, **84% of people trust online reviews** as much as personal recommendations, and 7 out of 10 consumers will leave a review for a business **if they are asked to do so**.

In terms of specific statistics for businesses in the United States, the following data may be of interest:

- A study by ReviewTrackers found that a 1-star increase in a business's average rating on Yelp can lead to a **5-9% increase in revenue**.

- According to a survey by Podium, **92% of consumers read online reviews before making a purchasing decision**, and a positive review can increase the likelihood of a purchase by as much as **270%**.

- A survey by BrightLocal found that positive online reviews make **73% of consumers trust a local business more**.

- A study by Spiegel Research Center found that a product with a high number of reviews and a high average rating is much more likely to sell than a similar product with fewer reviews and a lower average rating.

Overall, it is clear that online reviews can be extremely important for businesses. It is in a business's best interest to actively manage and improve its online reputation.

So, what if you could **stop negative reviews** before they happen! Would that be of interest to you?

Also, what if you could immediately send out requests for reviews as soon as your patient leaves the office? Would that interest you?

Well, hold onto your hat and listen up…

The program I have is simple, easy to set up and puts you (the physician) in the drivers' seat.

Once I set this up for a client, we first work with previous patients of our client to request a review from them.

When they click the link we give them, they choose how many stars they want to give our client. If they choose a 4 or 5, they get a link to go to the Facebook and/or Google page of our client to leave their review with comments.

However, if they choose a 1, 2, or 3, a message tells them we are very sorry they were not happy with their last appointment. We also ask them to explain what went wrong so that maybe we can work with them to resolve the situation and earn a 5-star review from them.

So, if they answer a 1, 2, or 3 it is NOT recorded on Facebook or Google or any other review site from our link. Of course, we are not preventing them from going to any of these sites and leaving a poor review themselves. Instead, we are working to manage a bad situation to make it a good one.

This way my client gets an opportunity to prevent a bad review BEFORE it happens.

This is so much better than having to fix a bad review once it has been published – then try to get the reviewer to take it down later.

At that point the damage has already been done.

Ours is a very PROACTIVE program rather than having to be reactive and always be in damage repair mode.

Remember a Good Reputation takes time to build, but a bad one only takes seconds to cause incredible damage to your business.

You now know how to Manage Your Business and Personal Reputation.

If you're interested in our program, send us an email at support@d14coaching.com and ask about our Reputation Management Program.

Thank you for reading!

If you liked it, please leave a review on Amazon for me.

May God Bless You and Your Business!

David DeSchoolmeester

Five-time #1 Best-Selling Author,
Speaker,
Certified Business Performance Coach,
Certified Open AI ChatGPT Expert,
and Founder of D14 Coaching LLC

https://D14Coaching.com

support@D14Coaching.com

Dr. E. Gaylon McCollough
McCollough Plastic Surgery

It has been a pleasure working with David DeSchoolmeester on a couple of projects. David has the technical skills and insight into how to best deliver one's message to the masses.

Mike Wingfield
5 Talents Financial, Inc.

After speaking with David about his services I'm convinced he's the coach I want to help me grow my business. I look forward to my continued relationship with David and I would strongly encourage anyone who has a great desire to grow their business to visit with David. His well thought out and concise plan, specifically developed for me, is spot on.

INCREDIBLE OFFER!!!

For Busy Professionals...

Would You Like Me To Personally Provide You A Plan Designed to Double *Your* Practice
...For *Free?*

From The Desk Of:
David DeSchoolmeester
Long Beach, MS.

Dear Friend,

I'm looking for "dream" clients that I **can bring in massive windfalls for.**

If that's you, **I will personally work with you one-on-one in your business to develop a plan designed to double your revenue over the next

12 to 18 months.

You Pay Nothing Out Of Pocket For This Initial Plan!

Here's why.

The first thing I'm going to do for you is to personally help you create a strategic plan to **bring in more qualified leads.**

There's no charge for this initial collaborative project.

At the end of this initial planning session **one of these three things will happen:**

1. **You love the plan** and decide to implement it on your own. If this is the case, I'll wish you the best of luck and *ask that you keep in touch with me to let me know how you're doing.*

2. **You love the plan and ask to become one of my Private Clients so I can personally help you execute, maximize, and profit from it and**

future plans.

If that's the case, we'll knock it out of the park ...And that's a promise. I've never had an unhappy client!

3. In the unlikely and *unprecedented* event that you feel like you wasted your time, **we will part friends.** No questions asked. Your time is your most valuable asset you have, and I respect that.

It really *is* that simple and there's no catch.

Think about this.

The "worst" that can happen is you get a new idea for your business and a new friend for "taking" 45-60 minutes of your time.

The best that can happen is we work together one-on-one to increase your profits.

That's Why This Is The Closest

Thing To FREE MONEY You'll Ever See.

Here's how it'll work:
We get together face-to-face, on the phone, Zoom, Skype, Google Meet or in person one-on-one and go over your business.

I take a look at what you've got,
what you're doing to get new prospects, what you're doing on the front end, what you're doing on the back end, and what you want to achieve going forward.
Once we have this "raw data", I help you come up with a strategic plan of action to **increase your lead flow dramatically.**

And like I said, *there's no charge for this.*

So Why Would I Make This Offer?

Two reasons:

First of all, I enjoy helping physicians keep and grow their practice.

Plus, it makes me very, very happy to see someone **achieve financial success (and all that comes with it) as a result of the help I give them.**

Second of all, it's how I attract new Private Clients.

Here's how *that* works:

Assuming the plan I give you makes you happy **...and you want me to continue to develop more ideas,** you'll probably want to continue working together long-term so I can help you implement them.

If this is the case, I might invite you to become a Private Client ...which is specifically built for medical practitioners who are very serious in taking great strides with their practice NOW!

The "fee" for Instant Credibility readers

is $1,500 a month (normally $2,000) ...but if you think about it, **it really doesn't "cost" you anything.**

Why?

Because I expect to make you much more than $1,500 from our first collaboration.

So, you'll see the value by the time we complete our first session - without ever spending a dime.

And look. If you don't want to become a Private Client, don't worry about it. *You won't get any sales pitch or pressure from me of any kind, ever.*

Now, obviously this is an amazing offer which you'll probably *never* see from any other "Internet guru" in the world.

Think about it.

I'm personally generating a profit-plan **for you** up front - *for free* - and *then* letting you pay me later if *(and only if)* you decide we work together long term.

Just tell me, and it's yours. No questions asked.

Who Else Would Do That?

NOBODY I know.

But I'm happy to put it on the line like this because **Private Clients love great results!**

Period.

My stuff works, and I know that if we work together, you'll be thrilled with the results we get in your business.

This Is NOT For Everybody.

Here's Who I *CAN* Help:

I'm VERY picky about who I'll speak with, and I've got a strict (but reasonable) set of criteria that needs to be met in order for us to proceed.

Here it is:

1. You have to have a solid practice already.
This offer is for people who are up and running already and simply want to take your practice to the next level.

So, you need to be in the $250K + range.

2. You must have a steady flow of prospective patients.
It doesn't really need to be that big ...just responsive.

(Finally! Size actually *doesn't* matter!)

3. You must have a good, solid reputation.
Everything we do together will not only **bring you more prospects,** but we'll be doing it in a way that creates **MASSIVE goodwill in your market.**

And in order for us to do that, you need to have your act together.

In other words, you need to be legit.

And finally...

4. You MUST follow directions. (Don't worry, I won't ask you to do anything weird.)
After all, if you don't actually implement the stuff I give you, we shouldn't work together.

That's it! Those are all my requirements.

Here's What I Want You To Do Next

If you meet the criteria above and would like to talk to me personally about getting you incredible results, then I'll happily set aside some time for you.

Here's how the process works:

First, you'll need to fill in an application.

Don't worry, it's simple and unobtrusive.

I just need to know what your current business is, get an idea of what you want to accomplish, and so forth.

Here's What Will Happen After That.

Once I have your application, you will receive a call from my office to set up a time for us to talk.

Our initial call will be between 45 and 60 minutes (preferably in person, Zoom or Google Meet – for us to see each other while we talk).

This is where we really begin working to figure out exactly what you want ...and how to **make it happen.**

I'll painstakingly review your goals ...and **I'll deliver a plan to bring in more prospective prospects.**

If you see the value in becoming a Private Client, we can talk about it.

And if you don't - *that's OK too.*

So, you literally can't lose.

(By the way - I've *never* had anyone feel like their time was wasted. EVER. That's why I can make this offer. I DELIVER!)

WARNING - TIME IS A FACTOR

This opportunity is extremely limited because of the intense one-on-one time needed in order to provide you with results.

Therefore, it is physically impossible for me to work with more than a handful of people.

Also, you should realize there's a very large demand for personal one-on-one coaching, and **what I'm offering to you is unprecedented.**

So, with that said, know that the window

of opportunity won't be open long.

If you feel like this is right for you, use this link, leave your application and let's talk.

https://D14Coaching.com

Talk soon,
David DeSchoolmeester

P.S. You might be wondering what you "get" as a Private Client.

The main "thing" you get is me.
Personally.

Like I said earlier, our first conversation together is FREE and it will be around an hour or so.

On that conversation we'll work out a plan **specifically for your business - based on what we talk about.**

You get that first call regardless of

whether or not you become a Private Client.

Now - if you **DO become a Private Client,** you're going to have access to me personally.

Here's how it typically breaks down:

First Meeting – Collaborative Meeting: The first week, we discuss where your business is currently at, what your long-term goals are and begin to learn more about each other to build a sense of mutual respect and belief in our collaborative success.

All meetings will be delivered in person or online.

This is different from meetings you've done before.

There's very little "conceptual" theory here. You're getting **one-on-one personalized** collaborative planning to help your practice grow.

After The First Meeting – Implementation & Continued Collaboration: The implementation phase is when we **"GET 'ER DONE"**!

The Continued Collaboration phase is where we come up with more ideas to implement and monitor our success.

Each meeting is LIVE one-on-one. So, if you have a question or need some help, **I'm here for you to make it happen.**

Review and Tweaking: We continue to do this in person or on Zoom as well because we'll be reviewing your business LIVE and helping you tweak plans to make it work better.

...**We can make it happen, together.**

We meet every two weeks!

By continuous monitoring, we see where you were last month and where you are now, a month later.

If you missed your goal (it happens to the best of us), we find out where the "hole is" and we plug it, together.

If you met it or **exceeded it, we celebrate!**

Then it's time to set the goals for the next cycle. This way - we're always moving forward. Growing and **making more money, experiencing more freedom, helping more clients, and having more fun.**

But that's not all. YOU'RE NOT ALONE! We stay in **CONSTANT COMMUNICATION**.

This way, I can see what you're doing and help you keep the momentum going between calls.

Always building momentum and seeing

constant improvement.

You should know that the reason I'm able to do such a good job and get such great results for my clients is because I only work with a small handful of them at a time.

As much as I'd like to work with "everyone", I simply can't accept more than that and still maintain the same level of service you NEED in order to **get the results you want.**

This is a genuinely rare opportunity.

If you feel like this is right for you, use the link below, leave your application and let's talk.

Conversations are granted on a first come, first-served basis.

https://D14Coaching.com

OTHER BOOKS BY DAVID

The Authority Maker

Amazon #1 Best-Seller in two categories (Online Advertising and Small Business Advertising)

https://www.amazon.com/dp/1502444291

We all know that everyone wants to do business with the "One Who Wrote The Book". Having Authority in a particular subject pulls in prospects and potential customers/clients/patients. This book will not only teach you the importance of Authority, but how to build it quickly to grow your business or practice. It is built on methodologies learned from several expert Internet Marketers like Frank Kern, Mike Koenigs and Dan Kennedy.

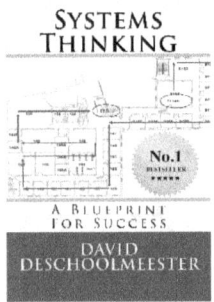

Systems Thinking – A Blueprint For Success

Amazon #1 Best-Seller in three categories (Business Planning and Forecasting, Communication in Management, and 45-minute Business and Selling Short Reads)

https://www.amazon.com/dp/1502392461

Systems Thinking is a unique guide to a successful business. This book is short, concise and to the point. You will learn some cold hard facts about business failure and what you can do to beat the odds. Systems Thinking will show you how the most successful businesses beat the odds of business failure and win long term.

Internet Marketing And Search Engine Optimization

Amazon #1 Best-Seller in two categories (Home-Based Business Advertising and Green Business)

https://www.amazon.com/dp/B00SUMNYV2

It is difficult finding someone who really knows what they are doing with Internet Marketing and Search Engine Optimization. There are many that would like you to believe they are experts, but they could very well get your website de-listed!

This is a short guide designed to aid high-end professionals to learn enough about Internet Marketing and Search Engine Optimization in order to intelligently hire the right person for their online marketing efforts.

Sleep Apnea Dream Killer

Amazon #1 Best-Seller in two categories (Physical Impairments and Respiratory Diseases)

https://www.amazon.com/dp/150230886X

A deeply personal story of how a Sleep Disorder almost destroyed my life. It is a uniquely true story of Sleep Apnea and just how devastating it can be.

Read Sleep Apnea Dream Killer and avoid the damage that ravaged my life!

In 1997 I found out I had Obstructive Sleep Apnea and began Continuous Positive Air Pressure (CPAP) therapy. I though my troubles were over.

In 2009 my Sleep Apnea "morphed" into a hybrid of Obstructive and Central Sleep Apnea and got a whole lot worse!

Read the devastating story of my experience and learn how to make sure this doesn't happen to you or a loved one of yours!

THE END

I hope to hear from you!

God Bless You And Your Business!

www.ingramcontent.com/pod-product-compliance
Lightning Source LLC
Chambersburg PA
CBHW052331220526
45472CB00001B/374